EXPLORE THE U.S.A.

MINNESOTA

Pamela McDowell

LET'S READ

AV2 BY WEIGL™

ADDED VALUE • AUDIO VISUAL

www.av2books.com

LET'S READ

AV² BY WEIGL™

ADDED VALUE • AUDIO VISUAL

Go to **www.av2books.com**, and enter this book's unique code.

BOOK CODE

Q781896

AV² by Weigl brings you media enhanced books that support active learning.

AV² provides enriched content that supplements and complements this book. Weigl's AV² books strive to create inspired learning and engage young minds in a total learning experience.

Your AV² Media Enhanced books come alive with...

Audio
Listen to sections of the book read aloud.

Video
Watch informative video clips.

Embedded Weblinks
Gain additional information for research.

Try This!
Complete activities and hands-on experiments.

Key Words
Study vocabulary, and complete a matching word activity.

Quizzes
Test your knowledge.

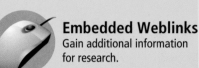
Slide Show
View images and captions, and prepare a presentation.

... and much, much more!

Published by AV² by Weigl
350 5th Avenue, 59th Floor
New York, NY 10118
Website: www.av2books.com   www.weigl.com

Library of Congress Cataloging-in-Publication Data

McDowell, Pamela.
 Minnesota / Pamela McDowell.
    p. cm. -- (Explore the U.S.A.)
 Audience: Grades K-3.
 Includes bibliographical references and index.
 ISBN 978-1-61913-365-5 (hbk. : alk. paper)
 1. Minnesota--Juvenile literature. I. Title.
 F606.3.M42 2013
 977.6--dc23

                          2012015079

Printed in the United States of America in North Mankato, Minnesota
1 2 3 4 5 6 7 8 9 16 15 14 13 12

052012
WEP040512

Project Coordinator: Karen Durrie
Art Director: Terry Paulhus

Weigl acknowledges Getty Images as the primary image supplier for this title.

MINNESOTA

Contents

3

This is Minnesota.
It is called the North Star State.
This name comes from the state motto,
"Star of the North."

This is the shape
of Minnesota.
It is in the north part
of the United States.

Where is Minnesota?

N

W E

S

Canada

United States

Pacific
Ocean

Atlantic
Ocean

Mexico

Minnesota borders four
states and Canada.

Many people moved to Minnesota in the 1800s. They were looking for land to farm. Minnesota was a good place to grow corn.

The railroad helped bring many settlers to Minnesota.

The pink and white lady's slipper is the Minnesota state flower. It grows in wet places such as bogs and swamps.

The Minnesota state seal shows a farmer and a river.

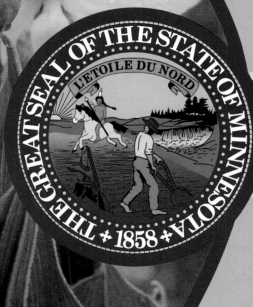

The state seal also has an American Indian riding a horse.

This is the state flag
of Minnesota. The state seal
is in the middle of the flag.
There are 19 stars around
the seal.

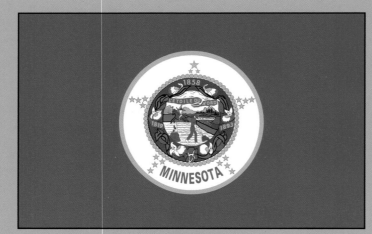

The large star at the top
of the flag is the North Star.

The state bird of Minnesota is the common loon. This bird is black and white with red eyes. Loons live near lakes and ponds in the north part of the state.

Loons can dive more than 250 feet under water.

This is the capital city of Minnesota. It is named St. Paul. The city sits beside the Mississippi River.

There are 331 bridges in St. Paul.

Minnesota is known for its iron mines. Iron is used to make steel. Iron from Minnesota is shipped around the world.

In one year, more than 40 million tons of iron was mined in Minnesota.

Minnesota is known for its many beautiful lakes. People from all over the United States come to boat, fish, and camp at these lakes.

MINNESOTA FACTS

These pages provide detailed information that expands on the interesting facts found in the book. These pages are intended to be used by adults as a learning support to help young readers round out their knowledge of each state in the *Explore the U.S.A.* series.

Pages 4–5

Minnesota's motto is *L'Etoile du Nord*. This is French for "Star of the North." Minnesota has other nicknames, such as the Gopher State. It is also called the Bread and Butter State and the Land of 10,000 Lakes. Minnesota has more than 90,000 miles (145,000 kilometers) of shoreline along its lakes and rivers. This is more than California, Florida, and Hawai'i combined.

Pages 6–7

On May 11, 1858, Minnesota became the 32nd state to join the United States. Minnesota shares its borders with Wisconsin, Iowa, South Dakota, and North Dakota. In the north, Minnesota is bordered by Canada. Lake Superior also makes up part of Minnesota's northern border with Michigan.

Pages 8–9

Settlers rushed to claim land in Minnesota during the 1800s. From 1853 to 1857, the population of the state grew from 40,000 to 150,000. Farming, lumber, and flour milling became important industries for the state. In 1883, the people of Minnesota celebrated the completion of the Northern Pacific Railway from St. Paul to the west coast of Washington.

Pages 10–11

The pink and white lady's slipper is a rare and delicate wildflower. It takes 16 years for the plant to grow its first flower. The lady's slipper may live up to 50 years and grow up to 4 feet (1.2 meters) tall. The farmer on the state seal symbolizes the importance of agriculture to Minnesota, and the river represents the importance of rivers to many of the state's industries. The American Indian represents the state's Indian heritage.

Pages 12–13

There are 19 stars around the state seal on Minnesota's flag. These stars symbolize that Minnesota was the 19th state to join the United States after the original 13 states. The largest star located at the top of the seal represents Minnesota. State laws dictate that the state flag should always fly below the United States flag.

Pages 14–15

About 12,000 loons live in Minnesota during the summer. They fly as far south as Florida during winter. Male and female loons take turns sitting on their eggs. The parents may carry the young on their backs to protect them from fish and turtles. The common loon has been known to dive up to 250 feet (76 m) underwater to catch fish.

Pages 16–17

St. Paul has more than 285,000 residents. It is next to the city of Minneapolis. These two cities are called the Twin Cities. The Twin Cities metropolitan area is home to more than 3.3 million people. These cities form an important transportation hub. The Minneapolis-St. Paul International Airport serves about 30 million travelers each year.

Pages 18–19

Minnesota has some of the richest deposits of iron ore in the world, and it is the largest producer of iron ore in the United States. Iron ore is mined from both underground and open-pit mines. The iron ore mined in Minnesota is called taconite. It is processed into pellets and then shipped to steel mills around the world.

Pages 20–21

Minnesota is known as the Land of 10,000 Lakes, but there are actually more than 12,000 lakes. These lakes, along with the many state parks, attract visitors from all over the United States. Waterskiing was invented on Lake Pepin in 1922. People visit the state for outdoor activities such as hiking, fishing, and cross country skiing.

KEY WORDS

Research has shown that as much as 65 percent of all written material published in English is made up of 300 words. These 300 words cannot be taught using pictures or learned by sounding them out. They must be recognized by sight. This book contains 63 common sight words to help young readers improve their reading fluency and comprehension. This book also teaches young readers several important content words, such as proper nouns. These words are paired with pictures to aid in learning and improve understanding.

Page	Sight Words First Appearance
4	comes, from, is, it, name, of, state, the, this
7	and, four, in, part, where
8	a, farm, for, good, grow, land, many, moved, people, place, they, to, was, were
11	also, as, American, an, has, Indian, shows, such, river, white
12	are, around, at, large, there
15	can, eyes, feet, live, more, near, than, under, water, with
16	city
19	its, make, one, used, world, year
20	all, over, these

Page	Content Words First Appearance
4	Minnesota, North Star, motto
7	Canada, shape, United States
8	corn, railroad, settlers
11	bogs, farmer, flower, pink and white lady's slipper, horse, seal, swamps
12	flag, middle, North Star, stars, top
15	bird, common loon, lakes, ponds
16	bridges, Mississippi River, St. Paul
19	iron, mines, steel